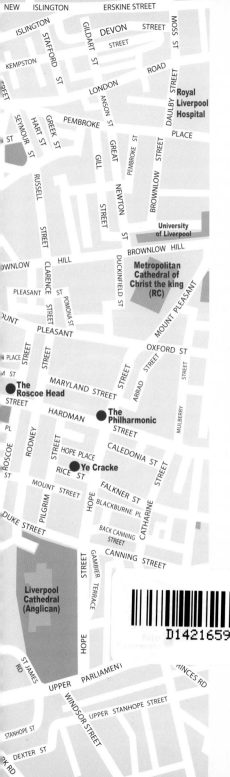

LIVERPOOL
HISTORIC PUB GUIDE

Front and Back Cover Photo
Peter Kavanagh's, Egerton St, L8.

Welcome *to CAMRA's Historic Pub Guide to Liverpool*

The Philharmonic, Hope Street.

*" Liverpool has
without doubt
the richest source
of traditional
pub interiors
outside London"*

*Licensed to Sell,
English Heritage 2005.*

Celebrating
Liverpool's Pub Heritage

CAMRA Liverpool and Districts (Campaign for Real Ale) have produced this guide for locals and visitors alike to help you to enjoy and appreciate Liverpool's rich pub heritage. A city's culture can be divined from its pubs.

Liverpool pubs reflect the city's growth as a great maritime and mercantile city, with pubs to match the confidence and prosperity of the nation's premier port. This history is reflected in Liverpool being declared a World Heritage Site by UNESCO and in being awarded European Capital of Culture 2008. Liverpool pubs are much more than architecture and bricks and mortar. They are a central part of the city's daily life and help give Liverpool its unique character.

*The Villiers 1970's
demolished 1985 see p54.*

More Than Just Architecture

This is not exclusively a survey of pub architecture. Rather it seeks to give an insight into the history and character of each featured pub, thereby creating a picture of our pub heritage. Each entry has photographs

Peter Kavanagh's, Egerton St.

taken by CAMRA members of the pub's architectural details plus a panel of interesting facts and a location map.

This is a guide to Liverpool's historic pubs, and thankfully most of them serve real ale, we have clearly marked these with the **CAMRA** logo next to the pub name at the top of each page.

It is an unfortunate fact that too many of today's pubs do not make the effort to serve real ale. Rest assured that CAMRA will continue encouraging those pubs to offer it, and provide beer that matches the quality of the pub. When you visit remember to ask for real ale so that licensees of these pubs will begin to realise that there is demand for it!

The Lion Tavern, Moorfields.

About the Guide

The guide has been researched, written and illustrated by Liverpool CAMRA volunteer members. The project has been financially supported by the Countryside Commission Heritage Fund, without which it would not have been possible to offer such a quality publication at such an affordable price. The project also includes CAMRA compiling a photographic and memories archive of Liverpool pubs. If you would like to contribute photographs to the archive please contact: pubs@merseycamra.org.uk

Enjoy Liverpool

Enjoy our Historic Pubs

Enjoy Real Ale

Join CAMRA

The Volunteer Canteen, Waterloo.

CAMRA The Baltic Fleet *Wapping.*

The Baltic Fleet is of mid-nineteenth century origin and was built on the site of a port and wine house. Its name arises from a Scandinavian fleet of the 1850's that imported sawn timber. Plans indicate that significant remodelling of the building has taken place. In 1901 the public bar ran the length of the pub in contrast to its current position. There were bar parlours in the rear of the pub. The "flat iron" structure gives the building the shape and feel of a ship and the nautical theme is enhanced by memorabilia on the walls. At one time, the walls were decorated with pictures highlighting West African exploration and links with the

Interesting Facts *about The Baltic Fleet*

- Its name arises from a Scandinavian fleet of the 1850's that imported sawn timber.
- The "Baltic" houses Liverpool's only on-site micro-brewery.
- Rumours have arisen suggesting the underground tunnels leading from the pub could have been used for smuggling goods or even people on to waiting ships!

world-famous Liverpool School of Tropical Medicine. There has been some speculation concerning the tunnels that are displayed on the 1901 plan. Their function is unknown. They may have merely been coal drops but it has been argued, albeit unconvincingly, that they have a more interesting tale to tell. A rumour has it that they were for smuggling goods to and from the docks but there is no real evidence they were used for this purpose or even reached that far. Equally unlikely is that they were used by the notorious press gangs to carry incapacitated victims to waiting vessels, as the gangs generally recruited in the street rather than inside buildings. Stories of ghosts abound but one of the regulars is a medium and has been unable to detect anything unusual. Finally, the "Baltic" is, at the time of writing, Liverpool's only brew-pub. The Wapping Brewery, so called after the street in which the pub is located, is housed in the cellar. Its beers are often named after adjoining streets.

CAMRA The Brewery Tap *Stanhope Street.*

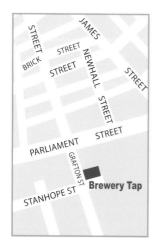

Interesting Facts *about The Brewery Tap*

- The pub was built in 1896-1902 for Robert Cain & Sons.
- It was originally called the Grapes, but became the Brewery Tap in 1990.
- When Higson's brewery closed, it was re-opened under the Cain's banner by the Brewery Group of Denmark whose refurbishment attempted to recreate a Victorian ambience.

The present brewery and public house was designed by J. Redford, architect, and built in 1896-1902 for Robert Cain & Sons. The pub was originally called the Grapes but became the Brewery Tap in 1990. The brewery and pub has an extensive red brick and terracotta façade consisting of various ranges and bays. There is much terracotta decoration, including beer casks, hops, barley and inscriptions – e.g. the original name of the pub. The changing patterns of ownership mirror the changing industry with several famous names cropping up. Cain's merged with Peter Walker from Warrington in 1921 but sold the brewery to

Higson's in 1923 for £100,000. Higson's had developed from William Harvey's Dale Street brewery of 1780, which was sold to Thomas Howard in 1845 and, upon his death, bequeathed to his manager/cashier - a certain Daniel Higson! After the closure of Higson's it was re-opened under the Cain's banner by the Brewery Group of Denmark who recreated a Victorian feel by importing a variety of fittings – screens, panelling, bar-back etc., the result of which is largely successful. There is a raised dais area with wooden partitions. The ceiling is high and ornate. The posters, windows and mirrors also add to the Victorian ambience. However, the overall result is not all authentic in terms of layout and organisation – e.g. the servery ends in a glazed hatch which would originally have existed only in a corridor, snug or off-sales. It was in 2002 that the current owners, the Dusanj brothers took over ownership.

Central Commercial Hotel *Ranelagh St.*
(no real ale)

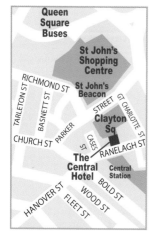

Interesting Facts *about The Central Commercial Hotel*

- The building dates from 1678, was a private house for many years, and when first used as a public house it was called The Albion when licensed in 1863.

- In 1888, it was renamed the Central Commercial Hotel after the railway station directly opposite the pub.

- Despite the less than tasteful remodelling, the pub retains a wonderfully ornate interior with cut glass mirrors and partitions.

At first this appears a strange building, for it has the date 1887 on the first floor and the date 1675 on the third floor. The earlier date refers to the fact that the site was previously owned by William Deane; a leading rope maker who lived here and had a rope walk out the back that stretched as far as what is now Queens Square. It was first licensed as a pub in 1863, when it was known as The Albion and the license was held by a Miss Smith. She was succeeded by Mr. Vines, after whom The Vines up the road is named. In those days the pub had a bit of a reputation as a seedy gambling den. In about 1873 it was sold to James Fairhurst who over a decade later wanting it to become a flagship pub opposite the soon to arrive Central Station rebuilt the place in some style with the present frontage. This is where the 1887 date comes in. It was done out in mahogany with 5 spaces including a large smoke room and behind it a small luncheon bar with a separate entrance on Deane Street, a street that used to run along the right hand side of the pub. As with many up market pubs from the era it also had a billiard room. Unfortunately just as this development was well advanced

Fairhurst died. His wife sold it to two brothers who completed the work and converted it into a 10 room hotel, which was renamed "The Central" in 1888 with a Mr. Hassall as manager. In November 1888 adverts started appearing in the papers stressing "entirely new management" and offering "hot dinners and luncheons daily". In the 1970s the separate rooms were made into one drinking space but unlike many pubs where all the fittings were simply removed, here the Victorian glassworks were put back in where they

remain to this day as one of the finest examples of pub glass from the period.

CAMRA Ye Cracke *Rice Street, off Hope Street.*

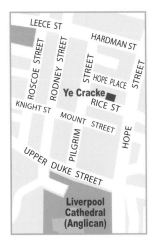

Not only is Ye Cracke one of Liverpool's most historic pubs but for many reasons it is one of the most unusual. The pub stands in a cottage-like building and dates from around 1852, when it was originally called the Ruthin Castle. As with the nearby Pilgrim public house it is likely the name was taken from a ship. Due to its size the Ruthin Castle's nickname was The Crack but records from around 1892 show Ye Cracke had become the official name. During this period the pub was famous in Liverpool for its singing sessions; groups of male choristers met at the pub to entertain each other and a drink known as a 'chorister' was available there. The pub

Interesting Facts *about Ye Cracke*

- Originally named Ruthin Castle (1852) it acquired the nickname "Ye Cracke" because the small bar held only 10 people.
- Although the owner Mr Randall added the adjoining house to the property in 1876 and created more space, the pub has retained its nickname.
- John Lennon frequented the pub in the late 1950's when he attended the nearby Liverpool College of Art.

extended into the neighbouring cottage some ten years after opening, creating the largest room and, to the rear, a narrow extension has provided lavatory space and a darts room. The bar position may have moved and the current floor was laid in 2004. Two internal rooms are of significance. The Old Bar retains the feel of bygone times and the War Office is a tiny snug where drinkers were banished if they wanted to talk about the Boer War. There are the pen and ink drawings of old Liverpool which adorn the walls of the largest room. Outside of the War Office is a small painting by the Beatle, Stuart Sutcliffe, which shows

him and John Lennon drinking at Ye Cracke. Lennon frequented the pub in the late 1950's when he attended the nearby Liverpool College of Art and it is said the relationship with his future wife Cynthia developed at the pub. Originally, a single row of approximately ten 'court houses' stood in the space between the rear of Ye Cracke and the rear of the large houses of Hope Place. The court was accessed via the passageway that serves the pub's side door and the street name plate 'No 1 Court' is still clearly visible today. Courts were overcrowded slum properties that housed many impoverished families. Disease and starvation

were rife in the courts and Victorian Liverpool had many thousands of them. Today a very pleasant flagged beer garden stands where No 1 Court, Rice Street once stood. The lower courses of the street-facing wall of the pub are clad with Victorian brown tiles.

The Crown Hotel *Lime Street.*

Interesting Facts *about The Crown Hotel*

- There has been a public house on this site in Lime Street since the mid 19th century.
- The Crown is yet another fine example of a Victorian gin palace.
- Note the ornately plastered ceiling which is probably the pubs most remarkable feature.

In Victorian times the Crown Hotel had a very significant status as it was outside Lime Street station and was probably the first pub that most visitors would see on their arrival in Liverpool. The earliest reference to a public house on this site is in 1859 and in 1888 William Clarkson of the nearby Midland Hotel took over the premises. The Crown became part of the Peter Walker estate in 1905. The architect is unknown but the construction style is of the lavish Victorian genre found elsewhere in Liverpool. The exterior has highly decorative stucco friezes and there are copper panels and ornate gold lettering. It is now believed that these embellishments were made after the pub joined the Walker estate as they are not visible on earlier photographs. The interior is impressive. The decoration is art nouveau and the plaster detail on the ceiling is particularly fine. At the turn of the 19th century, the upper floor contained a dining room and the glass cupola roof window is still present above the staircase.

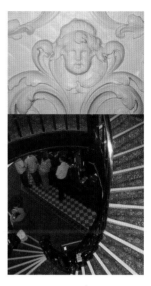

The Globe Hotel *Cases Street.*

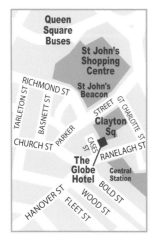

2005   1985

Interesting Facts *about The Globe*

- The Globe is one of the smaller pubs in Liverpool and was a Higson's house until 1980.

- The floor slopes disconcertingly upwards from the door. Walk the length of the bar and check out the height at the entrance and at the other end!

- The tiny back room contains a wall plaque commemorating the inaugural meeting of the Liverpool branch of CAMRA on 18th January 1974.

The Globe, which is situated in the city centre, was once a spirit dealer's premises but has been listed as the Globe since 1859. The current building dates from 1888 and has lived on to survive Liverpool's blitz, regeneration during the 1960s and the Clayton Square development. This small, two-roomed Victorian pub sits between Central Station and the Clayton Square shopping area. The front room is dominated by a fine wood panelled bar filled with gleaming brass and stained glass. The bar counter and bar-back may belong to the 1888 scheme or may have been imported but the fireplace in the rear room, the tiling in the entrances and friezes in both

rooms are original. Don't be daunted by the apparent crowding at the entrance which is due to the narrow shape of the pub. Just negotiate your way through and join the locals in friendly chat and a good pint of real ale.

A rather interesting feature is that the floor slopes upwards from the door. Check out the height of the bar at the entrance and again at the other end. This is likely to cause some confusion for those who have sampled one too many! This type of floor is unusual in a Victorian pub but in this case it seems simply to follow the lie of land. The popularity of the Globe makes it appear crowded in the front area. However, there is a quiet back room, which boasts more wood panelling and has some interesting 3D pictures of brewing on display. This tiny back room also exhibits a plaque commemorating the inaugural meeting of the Liverpool branch of CAMRA on 18th January 1974. The Branch has since celebrated the 25th and 30th anniversaries in the same room and hopes to celebrate many more such

occasions. The pub won the CAMRA/English Heritage Pub Design Award for refurbishment in 1996.

Ye Hole in Ye Wall *Hackins Hey, off Dale Street.*

Interesting Facts *about Ye Hole in Ye Wall*

- The pub claims (anecdotally) to be the oldest in Liverpool. It is said that the pub stands on the site of an original Quaker Meeting House dating from 1706.
- The landlord is reputed to have "sold" his customers to the press gangs.
- Hackin's Hey is one of the medieval lanes of Liverpool.

Ye Hole in the Wall can be found in Hackins Hey, which, in the past, was the site of several breweries. This narrow lane is just off Dale Street, which is one of the original five streets of Liverpool. Resplendent in crimson and yellow, it is said that the pub stands on the site of an original Quaker Meeting House dating from 1706, although maps and records suggest the Quaker building was further up the street. The date 1726 is displayed on the building, and the pub advertises itself as the oldest pub in Liverpool, although again this could be inaccurate and may relate to the date of the whisky merchants that once occupied the site.

Whatever the original date, there have obviously been many changes to the pub over the years. There is a curious set of fittings which make it difficult to make much sense of in terms of date. As you enter, you are surrounded by wood paneling the lower part of which may be 1930's, though the upper part is more modern. The casing on the columns in the servery area is probably 1930's. As you make your way to the bar there are two rooms on your left, one of which has a fine copper-hooded fireplace. Interestingly, until recently the beer was fed by

gravity from the cellar upstairs. There is also an interesting old telephone booth at the far end of the pub.

There is a placard inside the pub which recounts some of its history – e.g. the story of a seaman killed in a fight with a pressgang. It is one of the pubs that were ordered to hang out their lanterns during the dark months of the year, trapping many men into years of naval servitude.

More recently, it was the last pub in the city to open its doors to women after the Sex Discrimination Act of 1975

made it illegal for them not to do so. This led to the last piece of structural alteration to the pub – a ladies toilet!

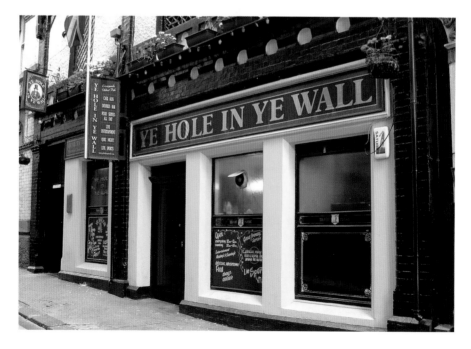

☆ The Lion Tavern *Moorfields*

The Lion Tavern is named after the steam locomotive of the same name that worked the Liverpool to Manchester railway before being retired in 1857. The Lion is one of only eight public houses in Merseyside listed in the Campaign for Real Ale's National Inventory of historic public houses. Its location on the corner of Moorfields and Tithebarn Street emphasises the railway theme of the area, which is dominated by the former Exchange Station. Inside, there are three discreet drinking areas, consisting of a long narrow main bar and two separate but essentially open rooms served from two hatches and a small doorway leading from the central service area. Above and behind the main bar is an ornately carved "C" confirming the association with the original Cains brewery that became visible only when several layers of varnish were removed from the original wooden panelling. The interior of the pub has undergone numerous changes since its original construction. Plans dating from 1903 clearly

Interesting Facts *about The Lion Tavern*

- The Lion is one of only eight public houses in Merseyside listed in the Campaign for Real Ale's National Inventory.
- The Lion today is actually an amalgamation of two pubs. The existing corridor layout dates back to 1915.
- There is a similarity of layout among the Lion, the Stork Hotel (p44) the Prince Arthur (p42) and the Edinburgh (Crosby) with a rectangular bar area and surrounding corridors. This was to facilitate police entry and exit.

show that the original building was very much smaller. In 1915, the adjoining licensed premises were acquired, the two buildings amalgamated and the existing corridor layout established. Externally there are few signs of this addition. Interior walls were introduced to create a multi-roomed structure, only to be removed in 1967 when the wooden floor in the bar area was re-laid. Further changes in 1978 included addition of wooden screens in the rear lounge and a dumb waiter. Uncertainty surrounds the construction of the splendidly ornate glass dome.

While structures to admit light in the absence of windows can clearly be seen on all existing plans of the pub, before and after its extension, it must be supposed that this structure appeared some time after the 1915 remodelling had occurred. Connoisseurs of local pub architecture of this period will notice a similarity of layout among the Lion Tavern, the Stork Hotel, the Edinburgh (Crosby) and the Prince Arthur with a rectangular bar area and surrounding corridors. Apparently, this was to facilitate police access to the premises

such that they could enter through one door and leave by another. In the 1920's the Cain's estate was sold to Peter Walker. Etched window screens bear testimony to this transfer of ownership. The current licensee merits praise for his restoration work, notably the glass cupola and woodwork.

Ma Egertons *Lord Nelson Street.*
(no real ale)

Interesting Facts *about Ma Egertons*

- Originally the pub had no gentleman's lavatory and men had to use the grid in the yard!
- Mary Egerton was known worldwide in theatrical circles and Marie Lloyd and Charlie Chaplin were among her friends.
- Actors who have worked at the nearby theatre are said to have enjoyed a drink or two in the pub.

Ma Egerton's is tucked away behind Lime Street Station and located opposite the stage door of the Empire Theatre. Ma Egerton's was previously known as The Eagle Hotel and run by Mary (Ma) Egerton – hence the name change. Although the L-shaped bar with its stained glass panelling is probably from a 1930's refit, the pub has a much older feel. Off to the side of the bar there is the screened, nicely upholstered lounge area, which is entered through a wide opening. The details of the upper parts of this screen are repeated elsewhere in the main pub area suggesting a unified scheme. The lounge is a room dedicated to the stars of stage and screen.

friends. The room is adorned with framed photographs and original paintings of those who have been known to tread the boards of the nearby theatre, and each of these is said to have also enjoyed a drink or two in the pub although this cannot be confirmed. It is difficult to imagine Marilyn Monroe with a pint of beer in her hand! A framed photograph of Ma Egerton herself is proudly displayed above the fireplace. This pub is well worth a visit, if only to see if you can identify the faces of the stars of the past.

Mary Egerton was known worldwide in theatrical circles and counted Marie Lloyd and Charlie Chaplin as personal

The Midland *Ranelagh Street.*
(no real ale)

Interesting Facts *about The Midland*

- The pub was bought in 1891 by Peter Walker Brewery from William Clarkson.
- The original curved and etched Victorian windows are still intact.
- The door for the Vaults has been installed the wrong way round.

In 1888 Green & Clarkson's Brewery Company Ltd, who brewed in both Burton on Trent and Liverpool, sought to raise £550,000 pounds to buy or lease 73 pubs. It is likely that this pub on the corner of Ranelagh and Cases Streets was one of them. On 28th July, 1888 what is now the Midland Hotel and the rooms above it were acquired from Liverpool Council on a seventy-five year lease. It didn't stay in this ownership for long. In 1891 it was bought by the Warrington brewers Peter Walker from William Clarkson. The pub is one of several that date from about the time that Central Station opened directly opposite. As with many Liverpool pubs from those days, it consisted of multiple small rooms with separate doors and the remains of five doors can still be seen today with the right hand one leading to the hotel above. The exterior probably dates from shortly after it was acquired by Peter Walker. Particular remarkable is the window glass, which is both embossed and curved. Like so many pubs of its era its heart was ripped out in the 1970s to make a single large drinking area, but many signs of its former splendour remain. On the two remaining doors the

names of two of the original rooms can be seen, although the one for the Vaults has been reinstalled the wrong way round. These are not the only original features to survive. Much of the glasswork inside appears Victorian. At the time of writing the detailed original layout is unknown but it seems likely that the bar has been moved forward. Looking at the ceiling gives some clues to the original layout but also emphasises just how much it has changed. The black and white photos show the interior in 1986.

Peter Kavanagh's *Egerton Street.*

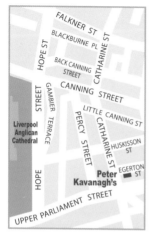

In 1844, No. 2 Egerton Street was termed 'a gentlewoman's house'. Ten years later it became licensed premises. At that time the place consisted of a typically Northern style pub layout – i.e. a drinking lobby with a room either side. The current building dates from the 1870's. However, during the 1960's the two adjoining houses – Nos. 4 and 6 - were bought and these were refurbished in the early 70's extending the pub to the size it is today. While the pub has had various names including the original, The Liver Inn, it has been called Peter Kavanagh's since the 1970's - after the licensee of the same name, who ran it for 53 years from 1897 and transformed it into the gem it is today. The multi-talented PK was an enterprising gentleman and alderman of the city who certainly left an impression. Peter Kavanagh was a creative designer. His plans for the many changes to his small pub are still displayed on the wall near the bar. Many splendid fixtures and fittings adorn the pub, most of which Peter Kavanagh himself took pride in designing and installing. For example his unique fixed twist-lock tables.

Interesting Facts *about Peter Kavanagh's*

- Peter Kavanagh was a creative designer and his plans for the many changes to his small pub are still displayed on the wall near the bar.
- The pub has had various names including the original, The Liver Inn, but has been called Peter Kavanagh's since the 1970's.
- Kavanagh frequently made fun of himself and it is said that the carved faces on the benches are caricatures of his face.

They have gullies which end in small central trays into which the spilt beer collects. (Some of these tables also were installed in ocean-going liners.) PK joked at his own expense and it is said that the carved faces on the benches are caricatures of his face. But his customers' visages

can also be seen staring down at you from the corbels of the shelving. Other carved wood marvels can be observed on the oak surrounds of the fire-places. These are taken from the original copper plates located on either side of the window in the Pickwick Room. And were uncovered only 8 years ago when layers of black paint were removed. The artwork in both the front and back rooms is by Eric Robertson and dates from 1929. It imparts both a warm glow and a sophisticated club-style atmosphere. The front room paintings are in the manner of Pickwick and the back room of Hogarth. The original sketches are held in the archives of the

Walker Art Gallery. PK wanted more light, space and atmosphere in his refurbished pub, so he had much larger windows installed. These are made of detailed stained glass and depict some of the city's historical significance, e.g. its shipping and its railway connections. There are unusual, large German lampshades which are made from a combination of glass, shells and lead and are based on the Tiffany-style of shade. There are other, unique items, such as the two bevelled fire fenders, which originally formed part of a wheel from the prototype of Stephenson's 'Rocket'. The stained glass and lead windows around the top of the older rooms and the copper bar all help to create a rich,

artistic ambience. The newer rooms, to the left-hand side as you enter, are filled with old radios, and other musical memorabilia. The exterior the building appears to be Edwardian but is in fact late Victorian.

☆ # The Philharmonic *Hope Street.*

The grade II listed Philharmonic Hotel is Liverpool's most famous architectural pub and has been described as the 'most ornate pub in Britain'. The 'Phil' was built from 1898-1900 by Walter W Thomas, the brewery architect, for the Robert Cain Brewery, whose "RC" monogram is set into the stonework of one of the gables. He also designed the Vines in Lime St. The name displayed outside the pub is "Philharmonic Dining Rooms"

Interesting Facts *about The Philharmonic*

- "The Phil" was built by Walter W Thomas, who also designed the Vines in Lime Street.
- John Lennon allegedly complained that being famous meant he could no longer drink in "The Phil".
- It stands opposite the Philharmonic Hall, which first opened in 1849, and is the home of the world-renowned Royal Liverpool Philharmonic Orchestra.

as the grandees of the Philharmonic Hall situated diagonally opposite did not want to be associated with anything as demeaning as a public house. The dining rooms themselves are upstairs on the first floor and are still in use. There are other rooms on the second floor where gentlemen's coachmen would have been sold cocoa as the Phil. was originally styled as a Gentlemen's club. As you enter the pub, notice the main drinking area which is a variant upon the usual theme of the northern drinking lobby off which various rooms lead. It is an important drinking area in its own right. The Grande Lounge was once the billiards room and since it takes up 50% of the downstairs trading area, this

perhaps indicates just how popular the game of billiards was in 1900 (c.f. The Vines 1907). Over the fireplace in this lounge is a plasterwork by Charles Allen called the 'Murmur of the Sea' and there is another of 'Apollo with Female Attendants' over the door. These figures are said to be based on a Mrs Ryan who posed semi-nude for them. The Phil is made up of several other rooms, including the smoke and newsrooms, now frivolously named Brahms and Liszt. Ironically, the Liszt room is now designated for non-smokers. The magnificent internal decoration throughout the Phil is a splendid riot of mahogany panels and carvings, plaster and copper friezes, stained glass, mosaic floors and glazed tiles. This intricate workmanship was made possible because many of the craftsmen would have normally worked on the luxurious liners built on the Mersey. The students and staff from the University School of

Arts and Architecture also helped with these decorations. Externally the Phil is a delightful jamboree of stepped and curved gables, pillars, balconies, turrets, oriels and other windows of all shapes and sizes, in the style of a Scottish castle. The magnificent art nouveau wrought iron and gilded copper entrance gates and the internal repousse copper panels were the work of Henry Bloomfield Bare (1900). The stained glass windows have a musical theme and there are two depicting Earl Marshal and Lord

Baden-Powell, who were war heroes from the Boer war which was being fought during at the time of building. The Phil is now a popular pub for tourists to view, especially the famous brown marble gents' toilets. Unfortunately, the rear part of the gents' has been sliced off – hence the mosaic pattern breaks off awkwardly. However, try not to miss the pubs many other exquisite details. Popular hero John Lennon has been known to complain that being famous meant he could no longer drink in the Phil. In 2004 the bar counter in the front bar was taken back to increase the size of the drinking area.

The Poste House *Cumberland Street.*

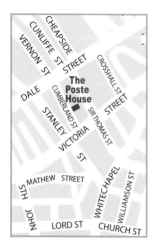

Originally a private dwelling belonging to a Liverpool merchant, the premises have been licensed since at least 1820 when it was called the Waggon and Horses. On the opening of the new Liverpool General Post Office in nearby Victoria Street in July 1899, the pub became known as the New Post Office Hotel. Since 1962 it has been called the Poste House. It is set in the business area of the city down a narrow street. The pub is small, cosy and friendly, with the lively atmosphere of a local. The room is dominated by the high-backed private, seating areas made of stained glass and wood. Other points of interest are the Victorian green tiling, located on

Interesting Facts *about The Poste House*

- While the Poste House was originally a private dwelling belonging to a Liverpool merchant, the premises have been licensed since at least 1820. At one time it was called the "muck midden".
- In its early days, it had a reputation as a haunt for smugglers.
- It is reputed to have included Adolf Hitler and Jack the Ripper among its occasional drinkers.

the right as you enter, a leaden tiled fireplace, situated near the staircase, and the large black and white photographs of some of Liverpool's proud stall-holders taken when the city's Victorian indoor market still existed. Perhaps the most noteworthy historical aspect of the Poste House is that this little old boozer was almost lost to us in 2002, when, as part of a multi-million pound regeneration project, it was due for

demolition. Luckily, after much staunch support from various quarters, including English Heritage, the local radio and TV stations, the regulars, and members of the Liverpool and Districts Campaign for Real Ale, the Poste House was saved. After re-consideration, it was decreed that the developers would have to build around it. Hence, there is a ready-made local for the new apartment owners to use!

Thomas Rigby's *Dale Street.*

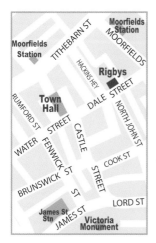

Interesting Facts *about Thomas Rigby's*

- There were buildings on this site in 1726 that originally included offices, bottling stores and the George hotel.
- Thomas Rigby (1815-86) came to Liverpool from the Newton-le-Willows area in 1830 as a wholesale and retail wine and spirit dealer.
- It is rumoured that Horatio (Lord) Nelson frequented a public house on this site in the 1790's.

Rigby's is a Grade II listed building, which is part of a complex dating back to 1726. The buildings once included offices, bottling stores and a pub called the George. It is adjacent to Ye Hole in the Wall pub (via the courtyard). The frontage of Rigby's, which faces North John Street, was formerly known as the Atherton Buildings but, in time, it became known as Rigby's Buildings. Thomas Rigby (1815-86) came to Liverpool from the Newton-le-Willows area in 1830 as a wholesale and retail wine and spirit dealer and gradually became the owner of a number of pubs in Liverpool. His prosperity led him to try his hand at politics

    ≈ (Lime St) ⊖ (Moorfields)

and he eventually became an alderman in 1868. Rigby owned this building from 1852 to 1886. In 1865 the decorative stucco facing was added. Ashby Tabb Ltd extensively renovated and refurbished the building in 1922. In 2003, the pub was taken over by Okell's Manx Cat Inns. who carried out another refurbishment. In the same year, it was runner-up in the Merseyside Tourism Awards' 'Best Bar' category. Rigby's is historically renowned for its food and in the late nineteenth century was described as one the city's favourite 'snackeries' with a reputation for Welsh rarebit and oysters. At various times, it has been frequented by anyone from pilots and stevedores to aldermen and councillors. The pub consists of three areas –one either side of the bar and, at the rear, the Nelson room – a spacious, square, 17th century oak-panelled room. The latter is so-named because, legend has it that Horatio Nelson frequented the public house on this site in the 1790's. A letter, allegedly written by Nelson, was displayed in this room for many

years but has long since disappeared. Today, the rear courtyard is used as a drinking area and has become popular with customers of all ages.

⬛CAMRA The Roscoe Head *Roscoe Street.*

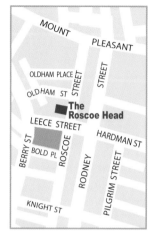

Interesting Facts *about The Roscoe Head*

- The pub is named after William Roscoe (1753-1831) who gave his name to the street in which the pub is located.

- A collection of ties once adorned the back room.

- The Roscoe Head is the only Merseyside pub to have featured in every edition of the Good Beer Guide.

The Roscoe Head is the only Merseyside pub to have featured in every edition of the Campaign for Real Ale's Good Beer Guide. It is named after William Roscoe of Liverpool; poet, historian and anti-slavery campaigner. Roscoe was born in 1753 in Mount Pleasant, the title of one of his better known poems. He was the first president of the Liverpool Royal Institution and was elected Member of Parliament for Liverpool in 1806. However, his career in the House of Commons lasted only a year. He died in 1831 of influenza and was buried in the chapel in Renshaw Street in Liverpool. The first collected edition of his Poetical Works was published posthumously in 1857.

The building that bears his name is a small, intimate pub is a converted house and offers a total contrast to the modern, prairie-style pub. It is arguably the best example in Merseyside of how a small pub could be divided up into a series of small intimate drinking areas. Radiating from the drinking lobby is a comfortable front snug, a rear lounge and a tiny front bar that must surely be one of the smallest separate drinking areas within any public house in Liverpool. All of these features contribute to its homely atmosphere. The pub was refitted in the 1930's and the screening and glazing is typical of the time. In 1960, it was run by two sisters and known locally as a seafarer's boozer. For several decades now it has been run by the Joyce family who should be congratulated on maintaining such a wonderful pub for today's beer drinkers to enjoy.

The Ship and Mitre *Dale Street.*

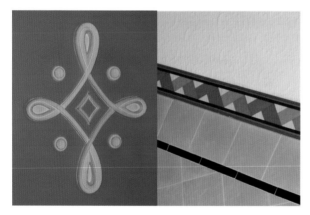

The name of Liverpool's premier real ale pub is relatively recent; the building only being named the "Ship & Mitre" in 1990. However, there is a long tradition of ale being served on the site with the earliest record being 1829, when it was known as Bents Brewery Tap.

In 1835 it was listed as the Mitre and that building remained until its demolition in 1934. The current premises were built in the art deco style in 1935 and the exterior still retains most of its original character - particularly the upper storey windows and motifs. The site

Interesting Facts *about The Ship and Mitre*

- The name is relatively recent; the building only being called the "Ship & Mitre" since 1990.
- It was the Bent's Brewery Tap until the 1968 takeover of Bent's by Bass.
- Until quite recently, areas of the pub were lit by gas lamps. Some of the fittings can still be seen in their original format.

retained its status as the Bents Brewery Tap (still called "The Mitre") until the 1968 takeover of Bents by Bass. The downstairs interior and bar lost its art deco styling in 1985 when it was totally renovated by shipbuilders giving it the current "nautical" theme which coincided with a renaming to "The Flagship". Only in the upstairs lounge and on the stairway can you still see the original, attractive art deco work.

The current downstairs of the "Ship" consists of an island bar serving two areas that equate to the forecastle and rear deck of a stylised ship. Both these areas were, until quite recently, lit by gas lamps. Unfortunately, health and safety constraints have meant electric light bulbs have replaced the gas mantles – although some of the fittings can still be seen in their original format. Flanking the steps up to the "rear decking" are two magnificent cast iron lamp stands which the owner has now restored to working order (again, sadly, these are now electrically lit).

A recent addition to the downstairs back bar is the full size mannequin of the television character Wurzel Gummidge – a sight that has caught out one or two unsuspecting newcomers!

☆ The Vines *Lime Street.*
(no real ale)

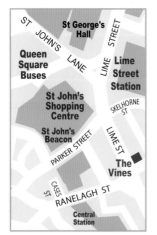

The Vines was designed by Walter W. Thomas (who also designed the Philharmonic Hotel) and completed in 1907 for Cain's Brewery. It was built on the site of a former pub owned by A. B. Vines, which was extended to become the 'Big House' which is still the affectionate name for the Vines. The red granite ground floor is surmounted by carved stone, topped with Dutch gables and its most imposing feature, a disproportionately tall stone tower. There are three storeys as well as the attics. The impressive outside clock is from the same company that built Big Ben. Inside, the Vines is designed as an Edwardian baroque gin

Interesting Facts *about The Vines*

- The original building constructed in 1823 was called "Richmond's" after the owner. Alfred Vines bought the building in 1867 and changed the name again.
- In the latter half of the century the billiards room was converted into the "pavilion concert room" with a glass dome in the roof and concerts were held every night.
- The pub is locally called the "big house".

palace with heavy mahogany pillars and carvings, plaster friezes and copper-work. The heritage room was used by Mr Walker (of Walker Cain, and the Walker Art Gallery) to display his paintings but recently these have been removed to the Walker Gallery for safe keeping after their enormous value was realised by later owners. The heritage room has a beautiful stained glass cupola and its own bar, but having been used as a billiards room, function room, and disco, unfortunately it is rarely open now. The size of the billiards room indicates the popularity of the game during this era (c.f. The Philharmonic Hotel, 1900). Some other notable features are, the cut glass windows - some of which have been replaced by etched glass following vandalism, - and the signs of the zodiac on the ceiling in the bar. Furthermore, there are two magnificent fireplaces set back to back in the bar and the smoke-room, particular features of which are two mahogany female figures either side of a beaten copper panel and also a coloured wooden relief of

a Viking ship. The servery in the large front room has been cut back to enlarge the customer drinking area.

The White Star *Rainford Gardens.*

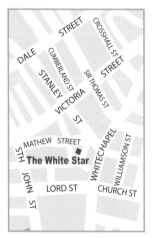

Interesting Facts *about The White Star*

- Just after the Second World War, a Mr Quinn bought a number of pubs in Liverpool and on the front windows he etched the word "Quinn's". Since then the pub has been known as the White Star (Quinn's 2).

- The back room of the pub was used by Bob Wooler and Alan Williams to pay all of their groups including the Beatles.

- There were no ladies toilets in the White Star until about 1987.

The White Star is probably unique in that it flies both the Norwegian and Czech flags outside above the door. This is a fine old small Victorian boozer with an elaborate tiled exterior in wonderful condition. It seems this is an unusual case of tiling being applied in modern times. The date of opening is uncertain but an advert in a programme from the Empire Theatre in 1887 reads "the White Star Carvery and Bar", so it was, it seems, going strong at that time. Inside, one gets the impression that it has hardly changed over the last century - unlike all other buildings in the Mathew Street area. Such minor changes that have been made have been carried out with respect for the quality and style of the building. The White Star looks as though it was originally a modest Victorian House, with a bar in the front room, a hall with a staircase to the first floor and a back room. The front drinking area is dominated by a large wooden bar that occupies about half the space. However, there are some seats with glass screens. Sadly, not all of the original glass has survived. A tiled floor adds to the décor and the radiators themselves are a work of art – note the figures at the end. As might be expected, parts of the walls are full of memorabilia of the age of the ocean liner - though not just the White Star Line. There is barely an inch of empty space on the walls, for, as well as the liners, there is an extensive boxing section in the hall and staircase area, a fishing section, as well as many photos of pubs in Norway and the Czech Republic with which it is twinned (hence the flags). The back room displays old pictures of the area, as well as a Beatles section. This is a genuine connection here, for it was in the back room that Bob Wooler and Alan Williams used to pay their acts. Also notice the superb Bass mirror in this room (signed J. R. Dunning & Son of London). The fixed seating is original and though the fireplace is not, the surround is. In the hall notice the newel post at the bottom of the stairs bearing the name of the pub. The cellar is unusual in that it is below high water level and used to be subject to flooding, but an ingenious solution designed by the current landlord, prevents this, allowing the beers, to be served in a first rate condition.

☆ The Prince Arthur *Rice Lane, Walton.*

(no real ale)

The Prince Arthur

RICE LANE   A59

A5058   QUEENS DRIVE

COUNTY ROAD

Buses from Liverpool City Centre:

Arriva - 2, 20
Stagecoach - 20, 21

Interesting Facts *about The Prince Arthur*

- The Prince Arthur is listed in CAMRA's National Inventory, bearing testimony to its architectural splendour.
- An interesting anomaly is that the gentleman depicted on the inn-sign is the Prince Regent rather than Prince Arthur.
- The pub shows clear similarities in interior design to the Lion Tavern (p20) and the Stork (p44)

Its location on a busy road outside the city centre in the Walton area makes the 'hidden' splendour of the Prince Arthur all the more surprising. The exterior of the pub with its deep red tiles and etched glass, hints at the delights to be found within. The coloured brickwork exterior would seem to date to the 1860s but the census of 1871 confirms the site had no connection with the pub trade at this time. The probable explanation is that the Prince Arthur, like most public houses, was not in the vanguard of architectural development and can be dated to the 1880s. An interesting anomaly on the sign is that the gentleman depicted is

the Prince Regent rather than Prince Arthur. The interior of the pub was refitted in 1905 and is similar in many ways to the Lion Tavern. The public bar is located in the angle of the building with a corridor surrounding the servery. Deep red tiles cover the counter front, corridor and dado. Stubby screens project from the counter to give a sense of separate spaces. The screen-work at the back of the servery mirrors the detail in the external windows. There is a drinking lobby in the expanded part of the corridor, where the tiling continues and those with the time or inclination may spot a small mistake in the region of the tiling. The lobby leads to the large smoke room at the rear of the pub, entered through double doors with additional etched glass which reads "smoke room". The carpet in the left hand corridor was removed to reveal the original mosaic floor. The Prince Arthur would be rightly considered an irreplaceable gem if situated in any city centre. As a humble street corner local it is little short of miraculous.

The Stork Hotel *Price Street, Birkenhead.*

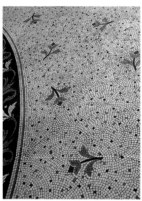

The Stork Hotel is a Grade II listed building that, in common with the Lion Tavern and the Prince Arthur, sits on a street corner with the bar occupying the corner and linked by a similarly shaped corridor forming a rectangle. Built in 1840, it retains many of the interior fittings from that time, including leaded stained glass, even if the original bell pushes for in-seat service are merely decorative. The extravagantly coloured Edwardian tile work and varnished woodwork in all of these pubs is similar, thus indicating significant remodelling at the beginning of the twentieth century (around 1903 in the case of the Stork). The

Interesting Facts *about The Stork*

- The Stork is the only Birkenhead pub listed in CAMRA's National Inventory.
- The pub shows clear similarities in interior design to the Prince Arthur (p42) and the Lion Tavern (p20).
- Particularly fine are the ornate circular bar's marvellous mosaic floor, the leaded stained glass and the original wall tiles.

public bar shows signs of a major refit. It is interesting to make a comparison of the Stork (and the Lion Tavern and Prince Arthur for that matter) with the Edinburgh in Crosby. All four buildings are similarly laid out, but the majority of the tiling in the Edinburgh was boarded over, probably in the 1930's, when ornate Victorian and Edwardian work was hugely unfashionable in what for many were austere times. The Stork's brewer was Threlfall's, whose house colour was blue as is seen in the tiling. This is worth comparing with the fabulously designed advertising mirror in the Saddle, Kirkdale. The colour scheme embodied within the tiling dates from this time (George Swift of the Swan Tile Works, Liverpool). A "News Room" leads off the corridor (compare with the Lion, where the partitions have been removed) and there is an elaborately furnished first floor lounge. In recent times the mosaic floor of the corridor has been uncovered, and the current licensees deserve praise for this and their general concern for the Stork's heritage.

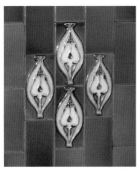

The Volunteer Canteen *East Street, Waterloo.*

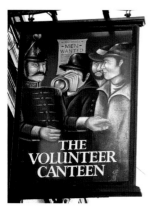

The first mention of the building in which the now "Volunteer Canteen" is situated is in 1827. Then the title deeds of the land occupied by the two houses to the south of the present pub state they were bounded on the north by the house of Richard Waddington. In 1840 he provided for the building of the Independent Chapel next door. This plot has long had a link to the "Volunteer Canteen" in how it was thought to get its present name. Entries in Gore's Directories up to 1868 indicate that the house was occupied by "Richard Waddington, gentleman". In that year the chapel was in use by the Primitive Methodists this was before the building of their Albert Road chapel. In 1871 the entry in Gore's Directory is "Richard Waddington, beer seller", but there is no name given to the building. The chapel was now the Waterloo Assembly Rooms after a short time in use as St John's Sunday school. In 1876 where the description in the directory is Richard Waddington: "Canteen Vaults" and the building next door is described as a Presbyterian Church, but subsequently to be occupied by the Waterloo Dramatic Society. Richard had died by 1888 as the

Interesting Facts *about The Volunteer Canteen*

- The building dates from 1827.
- The building has been used as a pub since 1871.
- In 1876 the pub was known as the 'Canteen Vaults'.
- The date above the front door is 1924, this is when the building last had a major refurbishment.

directory refers to Flo Waddington, "Canteen Vaults". Richard Wright, and "Canteen Vaults" is the entry for 1889 and in 1891 it has become John Waddington, Victualler. In 1913, for the first time, the present name "The Volunteer Canteen" appears. John Waddington remained in occupation until 1929. Why the change in name? It has been said that the former chapel was used as a Volunteer Drill Hall at the time of the Boer War (1899-1902) and there would be a ready supply of beer next door to quench the volunteers thirst after a drill session. Why it took another 11 years for the name change to occur isn't known. If you look up at the front of the Volunteer Canteen before rushing in for your pint you will see a date stone showing 1924. This is the last date the pub had a major

makeover and refurbishment and does not refer to the date of the pub itself. Note the Higson's windows which appear to date from this period. Inside the public bar to the right of the pub it is also true that little has changed. There is a new bar top and new display cases. The changes to the other side of the pub are more extensive, but there have been few major structural

changes. What is now the lounge bar was almost certainly a room off a corridor that gave access to a snug at the back of the pub as well as the lavatories, where only the glass in the doors seems original. The bar in the lounge may originally have been simply a hatch into the corridor and what now forms the bar may have been opened up later. Finally, note the bell pushes to attract waiter service which is prompt and efficient. Today, there is no indication of the former myriad uses of that plot of land bought by the first landlord of the "Volly" as houses have been built over it. Over the past 165 years the Volunteer Canteen has served the needs of the local community in a number of ways due to the purchase of land adjacent to the pub by the first landlord Richard Waddington in 1840.

The Scotch Piper *A5147 Southport Rd., Lydiate.*

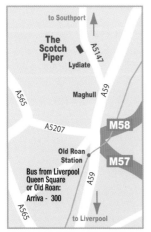

Claimed to be oldest Inn in Lancashire the Scotch Piper is on the west side of Southport Road, Lydiate, and with its fine thatched roof and old fashioned look it is quite possible to believe this. According to a recent archeological survey the Scotch Piper appears to be of mid 16th century construction. It is a two-storey thatched "yeoman" dwelling with a cruck frame consisting of three bays. It has external walls of brick resting on a sandstone plinth which may have been taken from nearby St Catherine's Chapel, Lydiate Hall or the same quarry that their stone came from at the back of Lydiate Hall. Crucks are a medieval form of construction found in the west of England consisting of long curved timbers joined together in pairs, rising from ground level and joined near the top by a tie beam or collar, supporting the purlins of the roof. Its centre chimney is built from hand-made bricks with fireplaces opening on both sides on ground floor level. A smoke hood is formed from horizontal wattle and daub supported on an oak beam and wattle and daub is found

Interesting Facts *about The Scotch Piper*

- The pub claims to be the oldest inn in Lancashire, being constructed in the mid-16th century.
- It was thought originally to have been called the Royal Oak and at one time it was known as the "Bag Pipes".
- It was one of the last pubs in Merseyside to use gravity dispense.

extensively in the construction of interior walls. The north bay is an 18th century rebuild of an earlier bay. Further alterations probably took place in the 19th century with the introduction of a new chimney in the north bay and alteration to the south gable. Following a major fire in 1985 timber from the middle bay was sampled by tree ring analysis and the date of 1550 has been suggested for its construction. The tree ring analysis shows that the trees from which the wood had been cut had been grown in open woodland. The still visible lower parts of the crucks seem to have given rise to the legend that the pub was "built around an oak". Based on the apparent date of construction as given by the timber ring analysis and the known fact that the property was part of the Lydiate Hall Estate up to its sale in 1922 it is possible

that the building was erected during the lifetime of Lawrence Ireland II of Lydiate, (died 1566) and during the reign of Elizabeth I. When the Scotch Piper first operated as an Ale House is not clear but it was probably from the mid 17th Century. Licence lists for Lydiate for the years 1663-1675-1681 and 1693 can still be found in the Lancashire Record Office in Preston. The licences were issued annually and were issued to individuals not for specific houses. Thought to have been called the Royal Oak originally, the pub was later called the Scotch Piper and at one time it was known as the "Bag Pipes". It was also known as "Old Lolly" but why is not clear, although the nearby bridge over the Leeds Liverpool canal is known as Lolly's Bridge. In 1922 when the Lydiate estate was sold, Henry Moorcroft the then

tenant purchased the house from the Weld Blundell estate. Mrs Moorcroft subsequently was licensee for a long period and it is said that she kept the small parlour at the North end mainly for here own use, customers only joined her by special invitation! In 1945, Mrs Moorcroft sold the pub to Burtonwood Brewery and retired leaving the management of the pub to Mr and Mrs Jones and then Mrs Orrin, Ada Rigby's mother. The Orrin's were in charge until 1961 when Mr Orrin retired and Charles and Ada Rigby took over the tenancy and happily continued until Charles' death in September 1996 and Ada's subsequent retirement two months later. The Scotch Piper was one of the last pubs in Merseyside to use gravity dispense although it now boasts hand pumps in the little cubicle which passes muster as a bar.

Other Pubs of Note *in the Merseyside area.*

CAMRA
National Inventory

Over the last 15 years CAMRA has been developing a National Inventory of pubs with interiors of outstanding historic interest. The basic criterion for inclusion is that the pub has been essentially unchanged for at least 30 years. The current edition (July 2003) contained just 205 full entries. Merseyside accounted for 8 of those, one of the highest numbers per area in the country. Those pubs are all featured in the Liverpool Historic Pub Guide. The Nook, Nelson St, Liverpool, (pictured on this page) is a recent entrant, unfortunately it does not serve real ale.

CAMRA
Regional Inventories

CAMRA is now compiling a second tier of Regional Inventories. The focus is still on interiors that are authentically old but the rules of absolute intactness are relaxed. Regional Inventory pubs are either largely unchanged in their layout and fittings or contain particular features of outstanding quality within a more radically altered setting.

Pubs under consideration for the Merseyside Regional Inventory include:

The Earle, Earle Road.
The Globe, Park Road.
Herculaneum Bridge, Dingle.
Great Eastern, Toxteth.
Boundary, Smithdown Road.
Royal Hotel, Smithdown Road.
Edinburgh, Crosby.
These pubs do not serve real ale

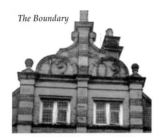

The Boundary

Herculaneum Bridge

The Earle

The Globe

The Great Eastern

The Royal Hotel

About CAMRA

CAMRA means Real Ale and Real Pubs.

The Campaign for Real Ale is Europe's most successful consumer organisation

Liverpool Beer Festival, RC Cathedral Crypt.

Established in 1971, CAMRA saved real ale from oblivion when a tide of tasteless, gassy processed keg beer swept across Britain. CAMRA led a beer revolution in which regional and micro craft breweries expanded to serve the growing real ale market. Now with over 75000 members, CAMRA is the national voice for beer drinkers seeking the flavour and quality of real ale. Additionally it campaigns to protect traditional pubs and to raise awareness of our unique pub heritage. Liverpool CAMRA produces Mersey Ale, a colour magazine, distributed free in local pubs.

Why Drink Real Ale?

The Short Answer is Taste and Quality.

Real Ale is the Premier Cru of the beer world

Real Ale is a living artisan crafted beer, full flavoured with a natural conditioning and liveliness. In contrast keg and smoothflow are dead processed beers which need gas added to them.

Real Ale (also known as cask conditioned) is the name for a draught or bottled beer brewed from traditional ingredients, and matured by secondary fermentation, either in the cask or bottle from which it is dispensed, and served without

the use of extraneous carbon dioxide and nitrogen.

In the pub real ale is usually served through a hand pump, although you may also find it served by gravity direct from the cask or by an electric pump. Always ask for real ale/cask conditioned beer. Real Ale can also be found in the bottle. Look for the words "bottle conditioned" on the label.

Why not enjoy one of the world's great drinks in one of Liverpool's great historic pubs. Join CAMRA and help to promote Real Ale and Real Pubs. There are many benefits of joining, including discounts on publications and FREE or reduced entry to over 140 UK beer festivals.

Details of how to join CAMRA and benefits of joining are on page 55 of this guide.

Merseyside currently has eight real ale breweries

Canavans
Barclay Bus. Pk., Liverpool, L9 7AU

Southport
Russell Road, Southport, PR9 7RF

Cambrinus
Home Farm, Knowsley, L34 4AQ

Station House
Meadow Ln. Ind. Pk., Ellesmere Port, CH65 4TY

George Wright
Diamond Bus Pk., Rainford, WA11 8LU

Cains
Stanhope Street, Liverpool, L8 5XJ

Higsons
Website: www.higsonsbrewery.co.uk

Wapping
33 Wapping, Liverpool, L1 8DQ

This guide is work in progress. It presents the best of CAMRA's knowledge on the pubs at the time of publication. If you have any additional information please send it to pubs@merseycamra.org.uk

Pubs Under Threat

Now you see it   *...now you don't.*

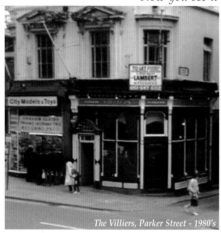

The Villiers, Parker Street - 1980's

" Nationally one pub closes every weekday, often due to development pressures. 26 pubs are closed every month, and 8 out of 10 of those are demolished or converted into houses."

CAMRA research

The Vernon, Dale Street

The message is that our pubs are under threat – both in our cities and in the countryside. Many pubs are worth more as development sites or as houses. In Liverpool we have lost a substantial number of pubs across the city, many due to the financial lure of development schemes.

The Vernon, Dale Street, a Good Beer Guide pub, and the Belvedere, Sugnall Street, a

The Belvedere, Sugnall Street